RECONNECTING MY BROKENNESS:
TIPS TO RENEW YOUR MIND

90-DAY DEVOTIONAL

ASHLEY MONIQUE

WESTBOW
PRESS®
A DIVISION OF THOMAS NELSON
& ZONDERVAN

WestBow Press books may be ordered through booksellers or by contacting:

WestBow Press
A Division of Thomas Nelson & Zondervan
1663 Liberty Drive
Bloomington, IN 47403
www.westbowpress.com
1 (866) 928-1240

Scripture quotations are taken from the King James Version of the Bible.

ISBN: 978-1-9736-6856-5 (sc)
ISBN: 978-1-9736-6855-8 (e)

Print information available on the last page.

WestBow Press rev. date: 07/24/2019

Ashley Monique
TheAshleyMonique.com

I dedicate this book to my parents and grandparents
for believing in me. You believed
in me, even when I did not believe in myself. Words
can not express how much I love and
appreciate each of you. It is truly a blessing to have you in my life.

Mother- Sylvia Watson
Father- Donald Boyd
Grandmother- Gussie Boyd
Step-grandmother- Gwendolyn Foster
Stepmother- Felisha Boyd
Stepfather- Ned Watson

Romans 12:2 King James Version (KJV)
2 And be not conformed to this world: but be ye transformed
by the renewing of your mind, that ye may prove what is
that good, and acceptable, and perfect, will of God.

You have been a sweet-smelling breath of fresh air
in my life. Through the sunshine and rain,
you remained. I truly appreciate you for that and
much more. You are truly my blessing.

Marquel Darrington

You have really pushed me into an upward mobility
within this last year. You encouraged me to
solidify and reach my goals despite the circumstances.
You helped to instill a confidence
within me to reach unconventional heights of success.
I consider you to be my mentor and friend.

Lisa Spears

PREFACE

At different points in my life, I lived through different stages of brokenness. Experiencing depression, a cancer scare, domestic violence, suicidal ideations, low self-esteem, divorce, mistreatment, molestation, abduction, being broke, unloved, used, cheated and hurt were all situations and feelings that contributed to the shattering of my broken pieces. The slow crumbling of my overall being since a child, took me to a dark place in life. I felt alone in this world. I felt as though no one could understand what I was going through. I wanted to give up constantly. I could not handle the negativity that was being thrown my way. The constant hurt and pain inflicted upon me, created turmoil and unexplainable brokenness that I could not shake.

Never would I have ever imagined that I would be abducted at any point in my life. No matter how hard I fought and cried, the car continued to drive away with me in it. I was taken to the country and held for hours, in an undisclosed location. My mind was very cloudy, and my heart continuously raced. Throughout the entire experience, so many words were said to me by my abductor. The only words that I can remember and still rings in my mind today is "I should end your life right now." Right at that very moment I began to pray harder. I called out to God for his grace and mercy to be upon me. Through this situation, God allowed my life to be spared. Almost instantly after I was returned to my family, depression and fear began to overtake my life.

Depression has the power to sink into every small crevice of your body. If you allow it to, it will take away your peace, sanity, joy and happiness all at once. Depression can consume your overall mind and suck every bit of life out of you, that you have to offer. I allowed it to happen to me. No matter how many great opportunities I was afforded, I still focused on the negative aspects of life; while in that state of depression.

I would constantly question God about why he allowed so many things to happen to me. There were so many things that I could not talk about with anyone. The things that had been happening to me in my life, caused me to be filled with anger and rage. I began to shut down and hold all my feelings within. My experiences in life shaped my actions and how I responded to others.

My mother so desperately tried to hide me from the negative deliverables this world had to offer. She worked two, most times three jobs to provide for her family. There were many times she made sacrifices, just to make sure I had the necessities in life. She wanted to maintain the pureness within me as long as possible. My mother wanted to raise a strong daughter, with the hopes of her turning into a magnificent woman one day. A woman that could be a successful individual, connoisseur, role model, upstanding citizen and child of God. My message to her is "I finally understand your mindset for how you raised me now. I appreciate everything you have ever done for me."

My paternal grandmother has a major impact in my life. She is always the person that I can count on for the continuous emotional support that I need. Despite the circumstances, I can always count on my grandmother to burst through the fire for the betterment of my good. Her hard labor in helping to raise me and long discussions given on making successful decisions in life, were not done in vain. I will forever be grateful to have her as my grandmother.

Out of the entire book, this was the most difficult section to write. Being transparent about the things that I have gone through in life, can possibly reopen unhealed wounds that I have suppressed inside of me. I am in tears at this very moment, as I sit here and reflect on the things that I have gone through in my 31 years of living on this earth. Some things I have shared with others and some things I will take with me to my grave. Being that I am a very private person, being so open about things that I have hidden for so long, may spark an uproar in others. At this point in my life, I couldn't be readier for that uproar, than I am right now. Sharing my broken pieces with the world may be the glue to reconnect the pieces for so many other people.

Despite it all, I have grown from a broken caterpillar, into a beautiful butterfly. I have gained an aura of confidence that is invincible. I have the mindset that will catapult me into reaching unconventional heights. I am aware that I have every tool inside of me to reach success. Those tools have been embedded deep within, since I was being formed inside my mother's womb. God has filled me with many gifts and talents. Occasionally, there is a personal shock when I reflect on the things that God has allowed me to produce. God does not make any mistakes. I had to realize that he developed a unique masterpiece when he created me. Yes! I have gone through a lot of negative experiences and I have had very low periods in my life; but I overcame them.

This devotional was created as an attempt to provide tips on how to change your overall mindset and thinking capability. This book will be the first edition to a series of devotionals. There will be a disclosure of intimate details of my life in each edition. This strategy is used to show you that an individual can experience turmoil and be transformed into a wonderful being of newness with the help of the Lord. The words from this very book is what helped transform me into the strong and unbreakable woman that I am today, thanks to my heavenly father!

Dear Lord,

Thank you for always bestowing your gracious blessings upon me. I will never be able to repay you for all the goodness and mercy you have shown me. I love you!

Your daughter,
Ashley Monique

DAY 1

Today is a new beginning for you. From this day forth, you will be the head and not the tail. You will be above the negativity and never beneath it. You will be the blessing in the earth that God has designed you to be. Get ready for the best days of the rest of your life!

- Deuteronomy 28:13 King James Version (KJV)- 13 And the Lord shall make thee the head, and not the tail; and thou shalt be above only, and thou shalt not be beneath...

Notes:

_____

_____

_____

_____

_____

_____

_____

_____

_____

_____

DAY 2

Believe in yourself and your ability to conquer all. God will impart brilliancy into your mind. This act will help you to become a genius and succeed effortlessly. Have faith in God and the process.

- Matthew 19:26 King James Version (KJV)- 26 But Jesus beheld them, and said unto them, With men this is impossible; but with God all things are possible.

Notes:

_____

_____

_____

_____

_____

_____

_____

_____

_____

_____

DAY 3

Capitalize on your strengths and don't dwell on your weaknesses. God loves you so much that he has gifted you with certain talents and skills that will help you to succeed. Appreciate what has been embedded inside of you.

- 1 Peter 4:10 King James Version (KJV)- 10 As every man hath received the gift, even so minister the same one to another, as good stewards of the manifold grace of God.

Notes:

_____

_____

_____

_____

_____

_____

_____

_____

_____

_____

DAY 4

You are unique and beautifully created into a wonderful masterpiece. Acknowledge your beautiful disposition with confidence and own it.

- Song of Solomon 4:7 King James Version (KJV)-M7 Thou art all fair, my love; there is no spot in thee.

Notes:

_____

_____

_____

_____

_____

_____

_____

_____

_____

_____

DAY 5

God will submerge and overtake you with blessings if you are a giver in his kingdom. Serving others is commendable in the eye sight of the creator. Be a blessing to others.

- Luke 6:38 King James Version (KJV)- 38 Give, and it shall be given unto you; good measure, pressed down, and shaken together, and running over, shall men give into your bosom…

Notes:

_____

_____

_____

_____

_____

_____

_____

_____

_____

_____

DAY 6

God has created you with the strength and determination to move mountains and not give up. He has developed a "fight" in you that is untouchable. Cast out all insecurities and open your doors to greatness.

- Isaiah 41:10 King James Version (KJV)- 10 Fear thou not; for I am with thee: be not dismayed; for I am thy God: I will strengthen thee; yea, I will help thee; yea, I will uphold thee with the right hand of my righteousness.

Notes:

_____

_____

_____

_____

_____

_____

_____

_____

_____

DAY 7

Your wonderful father has gifted you with the ability to speak prosperity into your life. Words spoken out of your mouth brings forth manifestations and results. Take advantage of this blessing and recognize the power that lies within your tongue.

- Proverbs 18:21 King James Version (KJV)- 21 Death and life are in the power of the tongue: and they that love it shall eat the fruit thereof.

Notes:

_____

_____

_____

_____

_____

_____

_____

_____

_____

_____

DAY 8

You are a gifted force of nature. God will give you favor and place certain people in your life, that will see the greatness in you. God will use those people to bless you and contribute to your success.

- Jeremiah 29:11 King James Version (KJV)- 11 For I know the thoughts that I think toward you, saith the Lord, thoughts of peace, and not of evil, to give you an expected end.

Notes:

_____

_____

_____

_____

_____

_____

_____

_____

_____

DAY 9

Do you know how amazing you are? God created you for a purpose. He designated exceptional abilities and skills specifically for you. Nobody else in the entire world can obtain what God has exclusively ordained for you.

- Proverbs 19:21 King James Version (KJV)- 21 There are many devices in a man's heart; nevertheless the counsel of the Lord, that shall stand.

Notes:

_____

_____

_____

_____

_____

_____

_____

_____

_____

_____

DAY 10

The dreams and desires that God placed on the inside of you were given to you for a reason. It is not by accident that you have desires to accomplish certain things in life. God is waiting on you to take the steps to put those dreams into fruition.

- Philippians 4:13 King James Version (KJV)- 13 I can do all things through Christ which strengtheneth me.

Notes:

_____

_____

_____

_____

_____

_____

_____

_____

_____

_____

DAY 11

God wants to use you for his glory. He predestined you to do great things. Do not be fearful to live in your destiny and calling.

- 2 Timothy 1:9 King James Version (KJV)- 9 Who hath saved us, and called us with an holy calling, not according to our works, but according to his own purpose and grace, which was given us in Christ Jesus before the world began.

Notes:

_____

_____

_____

_____

_____

_____

_____

_____

_____

_____

_____

DAY 12

You are blessed! Be proud and not afraid to tell others about the blessings that God has bestowed upon you. This will be evidence to others that he is real and capable of doing great things for them.

- 2 Corinthians 9:8 King James Version (KJV)- 8 And God is able to make all grace abound toward you; that ye, always having all sufficiency in all things, may abound to every good work.

Notes:

_____

_____

_____

_____

_____

_____

_____

_____

_____

_____

DAY 13

Stay focused on the plans that God has for your life. You may encounter setbacks and distractions but do not give up on "YOU." Fight to maintain the standards that God has intended for your life. Success and prosperity will be yours!

- Proverbs 16:3 King James Version (KJV)- 3 Commit thy works unto the Lord, and thy thoughts shall be established.

Notes:

_____

_____

_____

_____

_____

_____

_____

_____

_____

_____

DAY 14

God chose you! There are very few people that are selected and identified as being one of the chosen few by God. He has selected you to be a willing vessel and to do great works in his kingdom. He knew you before you were formed in your mother's womb. You are destined for greatness.

- 1 Peter 2:9 King James Version (KJV)- 9 But ye are a chosen generation, a royal priesthood, an holy nation, a peculiar people; that ye should shew forth the praises of him who hath called you out of darkness into his marvellous light.

Notes:

_____

_____

_____

_____

_____

_____

_____

_____

_____

_____

DAY 15

You are so amazing and great! Do not compare your life with the lives of others. Your journey to extravagance and eternity is different from your neighbor's. God will use you mightily for his kingdom, in his perfect timing.

- Psalm 37:7 King James Version (KJV)- 7 Rest in the Lord, and wait patiently for him: fret not thyself because of him who prospereth in his way...

Notes:

_____

_____

_____

_____

_____

_____

_____

_____

_____

_____

_____

DAY 16

You are beautiful internally and externally! The attractive nature that you possess was designed specifically for you. Identify your magnificent qualities and accentuate your unique assets.

- 2 Corinthians 4:16 King James Version (KJV)- 16 For which cause we faint not; but though our outward man perish, yet the inward man is renewed day by day.

Notes:

_____

_____

_____

_____

_____

_____

_____

_____

_____

_____

DAY 17

Have you been created in God's unique and perfect image? Yes! You have been set apart from others. It is perfectly fine to be different and stand out from the world. Count it as a privilege to be hand-picked by God. Grow to appreciate your position on the team of the creator.

- Psalm 139:14 King James Version (KJV)- 14 I will praise thee; for I am fearfully and wonderfully made...

Notes:

_____

_____

_____

_____

_____

_____

_____

_____

_____

_____

DAY 18

Righteous are those of the most high God, that genuinely live to please him. You have an anointing and covering over your life that is so powerful. That covering will push out all negativity from around you. The enemy will flee from you because of your anointing.

- Psalm 105:14-15 King James Version (KJV)- 14 He suffered no man to do them wrong: yea, he reproved kings for their sakes; 15 Saying, Touch not mine anointed, and do my prophets no harm.

Notes:

_____

_____

_____

_____

_____

_____

_____

_____

_____

_____

DAY 19

You are gifted and talented! God has already instilled all of the needed tools inside of you, that will aid in you reaching affluence. Do not demoralize the gifts and talents that God has embedded inside of you. Follow the course that your heavenly father has for you to reach victory.

- Exodus 36:1 King James Version (KJV)- 36 Then wrought Bezaleel and Aholiab, every wise hearted man, in whom the Lord put wisdom and understanding to know how to work all manner of work for the service of the sanctuary...

Notes:

_____

_____

_____

_____

_____

_____

_____

_____

_____

_____

DAY 20

God has created you to be an anointed being. Allow him to use you effortlessly. When you give God the first seat in your life, he will make things happen for you that others would not be able to imagine. Surrender your life to God wholeheartedly.

- Galatians 2:20 King James Version (KJV)- 20 I am crucified with Christ: nevertheless I live; yet not I, but Christ liveth in me: and the life which I now live in the flesh I live by the faith of the Son of God, who loved me, and gave himself for me.

Notes:

_____

_____

_____

_____

_____

_____

_____

_____

_____

_____

DAY 21

You are the apple of God's eye. He adores and loves you, more than you can begin to imagine. Nothing or nobody can separate you from the love of God.

- Psalm 17:8 King James Version (KJV)- 8 Keep me as the apple of the eye, hide me under the shadow of thy wings.

Notes:

_____

_____

_____

_____

_____

_____

_____

_____

_____

_____

DAY 22

Nothing will be able to hinder your prosperity. With the guidance of God, your steps will be ordered by the father. He will never lead you astray. Let God take full control of your life and guide you to richness, happiness and joy.

- Proverbs 11:14 King James Version (KJV)- 14 Where no counsel is, the people fall: but in the multitude of counsellors there is safety.

Notes:

_____

_____

_____

_____

_____

_____

_____

_____

_____

_____

DAY 23

God loves you so much that he gets jealous when you don't spend enough time in his word. Read and meditate on God's word day and night. He desires and cherishes a relationship with you. Your mere existence excites him. Doesn't it feel good to be loved that much?

- Joshua 1:8 King James Version (KJV)- 8 This book of the law shall not depart out of thy mouth; but thou shalt meditate therein day and night, that thou mayest observe to do according to all that is written therein: for then thou shalt make thy way prosperous, and then thou shalt have good success.

Notes:

_____

_____

_____

_____

_____

_____

_____

_____

_____

DAY 24

In life there is constant competition and team rivalry. Do not worry about losing or falling short. You are on the winning team. Following Christ qualifies you to be a winner!

- Romans 8:31 King James Version (KJV)- 31 What shall we then say to these things? If God be for us, who can be against us?

Notes:

_____

_____

_____

_____

_____

_____

_____

_____

_____

_____

DAY 25

Your body is a holy temple. Aim to be healthy physically, mentally, emotionally and spiritually. Taking care of your body is a way to show God that you really appreciate and cherish the life he has given you.

- Genesis 2:7 King James Version (KJV)- 7 And the Lord God formed man of the dust of the ground, and breathed into his nostrils the breath of life; and man became a living soul.

Notes:

_____

_____

_____

_____

_____

_____

_____

_____

_____

_____

DAY 26

God has created you for a special purpose. He has filled you with extraordinary gifts, that can only be produced and manifested by you. God has so much faith in you that he trusted you with his precious gifts. Magnify those gifts and use them for the kingdom.

- Romans 8:28 King James Version (KJV)- 28 And we know that all things work together for good to them that love God, to them who are the called according to his purpose.

Notes:

_____

_____

_____

_____

_____

_____

_____

_____

_____

DAY 27

God wants to use you! Be the willing vessel that he uses to get his kingdom work completed. You are the answer to a lot of prayers. The people of God has need of you!

- Hebrews 6:10 King James Version (KJV)- 10 For God is not unrighteous to forget your work and labour of love, which ye have shewed toward his name...

Notes:

_____

_____

_____

_____

_____

_____

_____

_____

_____

_____

DAY 28

Never give up on your goals and dreams. God will allow everything to happen for you in his perfect timing. Let him guide you on your path to success. Trust his process and have faith in it.

- Psalm 37:4 King James Version (KJV)- 4 Delight thyself also in the Lord: and he shall give thee the desires of thine heart.

Notes:

_____

_____

_____

_____

_____

_____

_____

_____

_____

_____

DAY 29

You are so valuable that your attention is needed by the most high God. He wants you to focus more on him. Let him overtake your mind, body, spirit and soul so that you can be filled with his presence. Don't be afraid to open yourself up to receiving ultimate joy.

- Psalm 16:11 King James Version (KJV)- 11 Thou wilt shew me the path of life: in thy presence is fulness of joy; at thy right hand there are pleasures for evermore.

Notes:

_____

_____

_____

_____

_____

_____

_____

_____

_____

_____

DAY 30

You are wonderful the way God has created you to be. Think of yourself as a delicate masterpiece, that is uniquely made. You are priceless and never forget that!

- Genesis 1:27 King James Version (KJV)- 27 So God created man in his own image, in the image of God created he him; male and female created he them.

Notes:

_____

_____

_____

_____

_____

_____

_____

_____

_____

DAY 31

Being genuinely loved is yearned upon by so many people. Being loved is so amazing. God completely adores you, more than you can ever imagine. His love for you is infinite and everlasting!

- John 3:16 King James Version (KJV)- 16 For God so loved the world, that he gave his only begotten Son, that whosoever believeth in him should not perish, but have everlasting life.

Notes:

_____

_____

_____

_____

_____

_____

_____

_____

_____

_____

_____

DAY 32

Speaking positive affirmations over your life will develop a positive aura over your atmosphere. Your words have power and meaning. Allow the words you speak to birth blessings over your existence. God desires the best for you.

- Mark 11:23-25 King James Version (KJV)- 23 For verily I say unto you, That whosoever shall say unto this mountain, Be thou removed, and be thou cast into the sea; and shall not doubt in his heart, but shall believe that those things which he saith shall come to pass; he shall have whatsoever he saith.

Notes:

_____

_____

_____

_____

_____

_____

_____

_____

_____

_____

DAY 33

Where you came from does not determine your destiny. The place where you begin, does not identify where you will finish. Reframe from allowing others to define your capability to reach success. God has formed you to be adequately equipped to flourish.

- Isaiah 40:29 King James Version (KJV)- 29 He giveth power to the faint; and to them that have no might he increaseth strength.

Notes:

_____

_____

_____

_____

_____

_____

_____

_____

_____

_____

_____

DAY 34

Allow yourself to be used as a willing being to assist and help others in need. Your good deeds are needed and will not go unnoticed. Do not grow weary in doing the great works of the kingdom.

- Galatians 6:9 King James Version (KJV)- 9 And let us not be weary in well doing: for in due season we shall reap, if we faint not.

Notes:

_____

_____

_____

_____

_____

_____

_____

_____

_____

_____

DAY 35

Praying to the father allows a relationship to be established between him and his children. Direct your prayers to the king and Holy Spirit. Through prayer, God will be able to build an effective connection with the people of God. He wants the best for you!

- Matthew 6:9-13 King James Version (KJV)- 9 After this manner therefore pray ye: Our Father which art in heaven, Hallowed be thy name.10 Thy kingdom come, Thy will be done in earth, as it is in heaven.11 Give us this day our daily bread.12 And forgive us our debts, as we forgive our debtors.13 And lead us not into temptation, but deliver us from evil: For thine is the kingdom, and the power, and the glory, for ever. Amen.

Notes:

_____

_____

_____

_____

_____

_____

_____

_____

DAY 36

Lean and depend on the Lord for he has your best interest at heart. Do not allow man to belittle your character and take away your happiness. The greatest joy of all comes from your creator.

- Psalm 37:3 King James Version (KJV)- 3 Trust in the Lord, and do good; so shalt thou dwell in the land, and verily thou shalt be fed.

Notes:

_____

_____

_____

_____

_____

_____

_____

_____

_____

_____

DAY 37

God wants to bestow gracious blessings upon your life. Everyone will not be happy for the blessings that will be trickled down to you from the father. What is meant for you, will be yours. Pull down your blessings and take advantage of the things that have your name on it.

- 1 Corinthians 2:9 King James Version (KJV)- 9 But as it is written, Eye hath not seen, nor ear heard, neither have entered into the heart of man, the things which God hath prepared for them that love him.

Notes:

_____

_____

_____

_____

_____

_____

_____

_____

_____

_____

DAY 38

Your path is ordained by your heavenly father. Let him lead you in the direction of the things that he has for your life. Seek guidance from God to determine the right way to go. You have been stamped and destined for excellence.

- Proverbs 20:24 King James Version (KJV)- 24 Man's goings are of the Lord; how can a man then understand his own way?

Notes:

_____

_____

_____

_____

_____

_____

_____

_____

_____

_____

DAY 39

You are worthy enough to receive all of the incredible things that life has to offer you. Do not settle for less than you deserve. Prepare your mind, body and soul to receive the blessings that God has stored away specifically for you.

- Ephesians 2:10 King James Version (KJV)- 10 For we are his workmanship, created in Christ Jesus unto good works, which God hath before ordained that we should walk in them.

Notes:

_____

_____

_____

_____

_____

_____

_____

_____

_____

_____

DAY 40

Do not allow contentment to find a place in your life. Always strive to become a better person. God will allow more to be connected to your hands when you take care of what you possess. Pinpoint your reach of prosperity and success as being limitless. Being mediocre is not what you have been created to be.

- Proverbs 3:13-14 King James Version (KJV)- 13 Happy is the man that findeth wisdom, and the man that getteth understanding. 14 For the merchandise of it is better than the merchandise of silver, and the gain thereof than fine gold.

Notes:

_____

_____

_____

_____

_____

_____

_____

_____

_____

DAY 41

Allow your mind to be filled and consumed with positive thoughts. Positivity can be a gateway that leads to happiness and joy. Be joyously contagious to others.

- Isaiah 58:8 King James Version (KJV)- 8 Then shall thy light break forth as the morning, and thine health shall spring forth speedily: and thy righteousness shall go before thee; the glory of the Lord shall be thy reward.

Notes:

_____

_____

_____

_____

_____

_____

_____

_____

_____

DAY 42

Make your decision today on which master you will serve. People leave this world everyday unexpectedly. Live by the commandments of God and be blessed.

- Joshua 24:15 King James Version (KJV)- 15 And if it seem evil unto you to serve the Lord, choose you this day whom ye will serve; whether the gods which your fathers served that were on the other side of the flood, or the gods of the Amorites, in whose land ye dwell: but as for me and my house, we will serve the Lord.

Notes:

_____

_____

_____

_____

_____

_____

_____

_____

_____

_____

DAY 43

You are never alone. Your father is there with you every step of the way. He will never leave you nor forsake you. God has you in his hands and you are well taken care of.

- Hebrews 13:5 King James Version (KJV)- 5 Let your conversation be without covetousness; and be content with such things as ye have: for he hath said, I will never leave thee, nor forsake thee.

Notes:

_____

_____

_____

_____

_____

_____

_____

_____

_____

_____

DAY 44

When you are on the borderline of reaching success, the devil will try to hinder you from reaching the finish line. He does not want you to succeed at anything. The enemy will throw stones at you to veer you off your destined course. Trust in God to give you the strength that you will need to endure to the end.

- Isaiah 40:29 King James Version (KJV)- 29 He giveth power to the faint; and to them that have no might he increaseth strength.

Notes:

_____

_____

_____

_____

_____

_____

_____

_____

_____

_____

_____

DAY 45

Establishing a relationship with God is very important. The relationship with your heavenly father is the best relationship that you can ever have. You are allowed to talk to him at any point and disclose your deepest desires to him. God's intentions for you will always be good.

- Acts 17:27 King James Version (KJV)- 27 That they should seek the Lord, if haply they might feel after him, and find him, though he be not far from every one of us.

Notes:

_____

_____

_____

_____

_____

_____

_____

_____

_____

_____

DAY 46

Spending intimate time with the father is so precious and pure. Honor God with your time, spirit, body, soul and overall life. Answers and guidance will be provided to you when you spend quality and intimate time with the creator.

- Exodus 34:14 King James Version (KJV)- 14 For thou shalt worship no other god: for the Lord, whose name is Jealous, is a jealous God...

Notes:

_____

_____

_____

_____

_____

_____

_____

_____

_____

DAY 47

Showing love and compassion to others is imperative. Loving based on conditions is not acceptable. However, loving unconditionally is. Love everyone no matter how bad they treat you.

- John 13:34-35 King James Version (KJV)- 34 A new commandment I give unto you, That ye love one another; as I have loved you, that ye also love one another. 35 By this shall all men know that ye are my disciples, if ye have love one to another.

Notes:

_____

_____

_____

_____

_____

_____

_____

_____

_____

DAY 48

God gifted us with the ability to pray abundantly. Prayer is a weapon. This weapon is always there for us to use. Don't wrestle with the flesh and blood, let God handle that for you.

- 2 Chronicles 7:14 King James Version (KJV)- 14 If my people, which are called by my name, shall humble themselves, and pray, and seek my face, and turn from their wicked ways; then will I hear from heaven, and will forgive their sin, and will heal their land.

Notes:

_____

_____

_____

_____

_____

_____

_____

_____

_____

_____

DAY 49

You can have anything you want and desire if you ask God in his name. Having faith, the size of a mustard seed will put you in position to receive an abundance overflow of blessings. Are you ready?

- Matthew 17:20 King James Version (KJV)- 20 And Jesus said unto them, Because of your unbelief: for verily I say unto you, If ye have faith as a grain of mustard seed, ye shall say unto this mountain. Remove hence to yonder place; and it shall remove; and nothing shall be impossible unto you.

Notes:

_____

_____

_____

_____

_____

_____

_____

_____

_____

_____

DAY 50

Fasting and praying brings you closer to the heavenly father. These acts of submission and discipline shows God that you are committed to fulfilling the will of God. If you want to see movement in your life, try this and you will see.

- James 4:7 King James Version (KJV)- 7 Submit yourselves therefore to God. Resist the devil, and he will flee from you.

Notes:

_____

_____

_____

_____

_____

_____

_____

_____

_____

_____

DAY 51

Obeying God is imperative for a successful and happy life. The ten commandments were established and created to serve as a guide to live by for the people of God. Use this guide to help govern your life.

- Deuteronomy 4:13 King James Version (KJV)- 13 And he declared unto you his covenant, which he commanded you to perform, even ten commandments...

Notes:

_____

_____

_____

_____

_____

_____

_____

_____

_____

_____

DAY 52

You have been selected and chosen. Out of billions of people in the world, the Lord chose you. It is an honor to be within the chosen few. You can do whatever your heart desires in God because you have been chosen.

- Psalm 37:4 King James Version (KJV)- 4 Delight thyself also in the Lord: and he shall give thee the desires of thine heart.

Notes:

_____

_____

_____

_____

_____

_____

_____

_____

_____

_____

Depend on God to produce your desired outcome. You are only strong when you are given the ability to be. Let God use you in every area of your life.

- Ephesians 2:10 King James Version (KJV)- 10 For we are his workmanship, created in Christ Jesus unto good works, which God hath before ordained that we should walk in them.

Notes:

_____

_____

_____

_____

_____

_____

_____

_____

_____

_____

God will accelerate what he instills inside of you. When he created you, his mind was set on developing greatness. Everything that you need is already dwelling deep within you, waiting to be recognized, trained and uprooted by you.

- 1 Peter 2:9 King James Version (KJV)- 9 But ye are a chosen generation, a royal priesthood, an holy nation, a peculiar people; that ye should shew forth the praises of him who hath called you out of darkness into his marvellous light.

Notes:

_____

_____

_____

_____

_____

_____

_____

_____

_____

_____

DAY 55

It is time for you to take your position in the kingdom of God. Let the king of all kings use you for his glory. When you acknowledge and obey the heavenly father, he will reward you openly for the world to see.

- Mark 8:38 King James Version (KJV)- 38 Whosoever therefore shall be ashamed of me and of my words in this adulterous and sinful generation; of him also shall the Son of man be ashamed, when he cometh in the glory of his Father with the holy angels.

Notes:

_____

_____

_____

_____

_____

_____

_____

_____

_____

_____

_____

DAY 56

The closer you get to your purpose and calling, the more distractions will try to overtake you. Distractions are designed to get you off focus. Don't let distractions hinder you from being successful.

- Proverbs 4:25-26 King James Version (KJV)- 25 Let thine eyes look right on, and let thine eyelids look straight before thee. 26 Ponder the path of thy feet, and let all thy ways be established.

Notes:

_____

_____

_____

_____

_____

_____

_____

_____

_____

DAY 57

Fight against negativity that tries to attach itself to you. Do not give anyone or anything enough power to take away your peace and happiness. God will bring you so much joy that others will wonder what has happened to you. The aura that you began to give off will be ever so pleasant and sweet.

- Deuteronomy 28:2 King James Version (KJV)- 2 And all these blessings shall come on thee, and overtake thee, if thou shalt hearken unto the voice of the Lord thy God.

Notes:

_____

_____

_____

_____

_____

_____

_____

_____

_____

_____

DAY 58

Your life and destiny are not an accident. You are valuable and needed in this world. Allow God to assist you in making your positive stamp on the world. Don't let your life be lived in vain.

- Ephesians 1:11 King James Version (KJV)- 11 In whom also we have obtained an inheritance, being predestinated according to the purpose of him who worketh all things after the counsel of his own will.

Notes:

_____

_____

_____

_____

_____

_____

_____

_____

_____

_____

DAY 59

God wants to be put above all in your life. He should be ranked first and foremost no matter what. God will allow your territory to shift so that he can take his rightful place in your life. Reserve the number one spot for him!

- Matthew 6:33 King James Version (KJV)- 33 But seek ye first the kingdom of God, and his righteousness; and all these things shall be added unto you.

Notes:

_____

_____

_____

_____

_____

_____

_____

_____

_____

_____

_____

DAY 60

Everyone has interest and desires that fulfills their heart. God has given us all 24 hours in a day. It's all about what you decide to do with the time that God has given you. Never give up on reaching your dreams. You can accomplish anything that you put your mind to.

- Psalm 37:5 King James Version (KJV)- 5 Commit thy way unto the Lord; trust also in him; and he shall bring it to pass.

Notes:

_____

_____

_____

_____

_____

_____

_____

_____

_____

_____

DAY 61

You were not created empty. God placed gifts and talents inside of you when you were created. Those gifts and talents were given to you for a reason. Utilize every ability that have been embedded within you.

- James 1:17 King James Version (KJV)- 17 Every good gift and every perfect gift is from above, and cometh down from the Father of lights...

Notes:

_____

_____

_____

_____

_____

_____

_____

_____

_____

_____

DAY 62

Being developed inside the womb and birthed into this world can be a difficult process. If you can make it through the birthing process, then be confident enough that you can make it through life. God will never fail you. If he allowed you to make it this far, he won't fail you now. He will always have your best interest at heart.

- Philippians 1:6 King James Version (KJV)- 6 Being confident of this very thing, that he which hath begun a good work in you will perform it until the day of Jesus Christ.

Notes:

_____

_____

_____

_____

_____

_____

_____

_____

_____

_____

DAY 63

Don't be bewildered when you are criticized by the world. God has a calling on your life. You are not called, until you are criticized and talked about. Know that you are doing great things when people start talking about you. Let them keep talking, while you continue to produce outcome.

- Psalm 110:1-2 King James Version (KJV)- 110 The Lord said unto my Lord, Sit thou at my right hand, until I make thine enemies thy footstool. 2 The Lord shall send the rod of thy strength out of Zion: rule thou in the midst of thine enemies.

Notes:

_____

_____

_____

_____

_____

_____

_____

_____

_____

_____

DAY 64

Where you come from does not always determine where you are going. Allow God to order your footsteps. The plan he has for your life is phenomenal. Your history does not determine your destiny.

- Proverbs 16:3 King James Version (KJV)- 3 Commit thy works unto the Lord, and thy thoughts shall be established.

Notes:

_____

_____

_____

_____

_____

_____

_____

_____

_____

DAY 65

No matter what, don't give up on your destiny. God will give you strategy in the pursuit. Do not focus on the critics and the haters. Pay more attention to your supporters and the people that you will be helping in the kingdom of God.

- Isaiah 41:10 King James Version (KJV)- 10 Fear thou not; for I am with thee: be not dismayed; for I am thy God: I will strengthen thee; yea, I will help thee; yea, I will uphold thee with the right hand of my righteousness.

Notes:

_____

_____

_____

_____

_____

_____

_____

_____

_____

_____

DAY 66

Surround yourself with strong people that have your best interest at heart. Allow God to give you discernment so that you can spot negative people when you see them. Keep your circle tight and spiritually connected.

- Psalm 31:3 King James Version (KJV)- 3 For thou art my rock and my fortress; therefore for thy name's sake lead me, and guide me.

Notes:

_____

_____

_____

_____

_____

_____

_____

_____

_____

DAY 67

Speak directly to God for anything you want or need to know. Having a relationship with him, will allow you to hear him and you will receive the answers that you need. Don't take permanent advice from temporary people.

- Mark 11:24 King James Version (KJV)- 24 Therefore I say unto you, What things soever ye desire, when ye pray, believe that ye receive them, and ye shall have them.

Notes:

_____

_____

_____

_____

_____

_____

_____

_____

_____

_____

_____

DAY 68

God has the ultimate say so. Don't be distracted or worried by things you can't change. Pray to the heavenly father and he will work everything out for your good.

- Romans 8:28 King James Version (KJV)- 28 And we know that all things work together for good to them that love God, to them who are the called according to his purpose.

Notes:

_____

_____

_____

_____

_____

_____

_____

_____

_____

_____

DAY 69

You are too brilliant to be distracted. God has need of you in this world. Don't hold up the blessings that are waiting to overtake your life by not getting things done that God wants you to do.

- 1 John 2:17 King James Version (KJV)- 17 And the world passeth away, and the lust thereof: but he that doeth the will of God abideth for ever.

Notes:

_____

_____

_____

_____

_____

_____

_____

_____

_____

_____

DAY 70

You can be a great influence in the lives of others. God wants you to be a willing vessel in his kingdom. Other people watch, observe and mimic you when you don't know it. Be the change that other people need to see to help change their lives.

- James 5:20 King James Version (KJV)- 20 Let him know, that he which converteth the sinner from the error of his way shall save a soul from death, and shall hide a multitude of sins.

Notes:

_____

_____

_____

_____

_____

_____

_____

_____

_____

_____

DAY 71

Does your attitude and actions portray you to be a good person? Treating others with respect and dignity shows good character. Be the sunshine and happiness that others need to see, so that they can be pushed forward in their day. You are admired by so many people. Love is a key factor in the kingdom of God that will bless your admirers.

- Matthew 7:12 King James Version (KJV)- 12 Therefore all things whatsoever ye would that men should do to you, do ye even so to them...

Notes:

_____

_____

_____

_____

_____

_____

_____

_____

_____

_____

DAY 72

Don't allow yourself to leave this world full of purpose. God has preordained everyone with a purpose in life before they were birthed into the earth. That purpose is based on what God wants you to do with your life, while living. Strive to fulfill your purpose before you take your last breath. Leave here as an empty vessel of purpose.

- 2 Timothy 2:21 King James Version (KJV)- 21 If a man therefore purge himself from these, he shall be a vessel unto honour, sanctified, and meet for the master's use, and prepared unto every good work.

Notes:

_____

_____

_____

_____

_____

_____

_____

_____

DAY 73

Being hurt by others is never something that most people want to happen. Whether your hurt was done intentionally or unintentionally, we must forgive. Forgiving others that have hurt you will unlock an overflow of blessings that God will bestow upon you. Forgive others and God will forgive you.

- Matthew 6:15 King James Version (KJV)- 15 But if ye forgive not men their trespasses, neither will your Father forgive your trespasses.

Notes:

_____

_____

_____

_____

_____

_____

_____

_____

_____

_____

DAY 74

You are a king or queen. You should appear, act and be treated as such. Your mere existence into the earth is utterly beautiful. God created a masterpiece when he created you. Love yourself!

- 2 Corinthians 5:17 King James Version (KJV)- 17 Therefore if any man be in Christ, he is a new creature…

Notes:

_____

_____

_____

_____

_____

_____

_____

_____

_____

_____

DAY 75

Being liked by everyone is almost impossible. Be yourself and don't change in a negative way to please others. You are uniquely rare. God created you for a reason. There will never be another person created with your DNA. Be the best person that you can be.

- Ecclesiastes 9:10 King James Version (KJV)- 10 Whatsoever thy hand findeth to do, do it with thy might; for there is no work, nor device, nor knowledge, nor wisdom, in the grave, whither thou goest.

Notes:

_____

_____

_____

_____

_____

_____

_____

_____

_____

_____

DAY 76

God has need of you! He reveals great things for people to do in the earth to his most trusted servants. Things that you do for the kingdom of God, has the potential to save the lives of many people. Do not take your calling from God lightly.

- Jeremiah 33:3 King James Version (KJV)- 3 Call unto me, and I will answer thee, and show thee great and mighty things, which thou knowest not.

Notes:

_____

_____

_____

_____

_____

_____

_____

_____

_____

_____

DAY 77

Being successful is something that a lot of people worry about being. God has a plan for your life. His plan is to bring you prosperity in the things that you do. God has the power to let everything you touch, turn to gold. Hearing from God and following his plans is an intricate part of your future success. Follow God's plan for your life.

- Psalm 32:8 King James Version (KJV)- 8 I will instruct thee and teach thee in the way which thou shalt go: I will guide thee with mine eye.

Notes:

_____

_____

_____

_____

_____

_____

_____

_____

_____

_____

DAY 78

Everyone wants to be shown love in some form. Love can be given through a parent, significant other, friend, family member, mentor, child, etc. No matter how much a person desires to be loved, only God can give you an everlasting love. His love is infinite among dimensions.

- Romans 5:8 King James Version (KJV)- 8 But God commendeth his love toward us, in that, while we were yet sinners, Christ died for us.

Notes:

_____

_____

_____

_____

_____

_____

_____

_____

_____

_____

DAY 79

God will hold you accountable for what you impart into the lives of others. He wants you to show and exert positivity into the lives of others. There is a reason for you being surrounded by certain people. Use your presence to be a blessing to God's people.

- Galatians 6:2 King James Version (KJV)- 2 Bear ye one another's burdens, and so fulfil the law of Christ.

Notes:

_____

_____

_____

_____

_____

_____

_____

_____

_____

_____

DAY 80

Your body is a holy temple from God. Your physical being should be valued and treated as a gift. Eating right, exercising and not abusing drugs is a few ways to show appreciation for the body that God has given to you. Your flesh will eventually fade away but handle it with care to maintain your health.

- 1 Corinthians 10:31 King James Version (KJV)- 31 Whether therefore ye eat, or drink, or whatsoever ye do, do all to the glory of God.

Notes:

_____

_____

_____

_____

_____

_____

_____

_____

_____

_____

DAY 81

Be patient and allow God to bless you. Your blessings and favor will come in the right season. God will continuously breath an essence of blessed air over your territory in his timing. Patience is a virtue.

- Psalm 27:14 King James Version (KJV)- 14 Wait on the Lord: be of good courage, and he shall strengthen thine heart…

Notes:

_____

_____

_____

_____

_____

_____

_____

_____

_____

_____

DAY 82

Petition God for the wants and desires of your heart. Anything that you ask for in the name of the father will be done, if you have faith. God loves you and he wants you to have the best there is to give.

- Hebrews 11:1 King James Version (KJV)- 11 Now faith is the substance of things hoped for, the evidence of things not seen.

Notes:

_____

_____

_____

_____

_____

_____

_____

_____

_____

_____

DAY 83

Use your mind to develop and create magnificent ideas. Giving God the freedom to impart intellectual knowledge into your mind, allows for growth to take place. Generate ideas of success. An idle mind is the devil's workshop.

- Proverbs 1:7 King James Version (KJV)- 7 The fear of the Lord is the beginning of knowledge: but fools despise wisdom and instruction.

Notes:

_____

_____

_____

_____

_____

_____

_____

_____

_____

_____

Your image should be a reflection of your heavenly father. Certain people should be able to recognize that you are a servant of God. Servants of God are considered brothers and sisters in Christ.

- Genesis 1:26-27 King James Version (KJV)- 26 And God said, Let us make man in our image, after our likeness: and let them have dominion over the fish of the sea, and over the fowl of the air, and over the cattle, and over all the earth... 27 So God created man in his own image, in the image of God created he him; male and female created he them.

Notes:

_____

_____

_____

_____

_____

_____

_____

_____

_____

DAY 85

The anointing that God has on your life can be very attractive to others. They will see the amazing qualities you possess, and they will want to be a part of your amazingness. Protect the anointing that you have been given.

- 1 John 2:27 King James Version (KJV)- 27 But the anointing which ye have received of him abideth in you, and ye need not that any man teach you: but as the same anointing teacheth you of all things, and is truth, and is no lie, and even as it hath taught you, ye shall abide in him.

Notes:

_____

_____

_____

_____

_____

_____

_____

_____

_____

_____

DAY 86

Leaving a positive legacy in the world is important. Allowing God to use you for the enhancement of his kingdom through helping others is a necessity. This action will help to create a legacy that others will remember. What do you want to be known for when you leave the earth?

- Proverbs 13:22 King James Version (KJV)- 22 A good man leaveth an inheritance to his children's children...

Notes:

_____

_____

_____

_____

_____

_____

_____

_____

_____

_____

DAY 87

Smell the beautiful roses while you still can. Having an appreciation of life can contribute to much happiness. Try to reframe from complaining about things that you cannot change. Be grateful of the life that has been given to you from God.

- Ephesians 4:29 King James Version (KJV)- 29 Let no corrupt communication proceed out of your mouth, but that which is good to the use of edifying, that it may minister grace unto the hearers.

Notes:

_____

_____

_____

_____

_____

_____

_____

_____

_____

_____

DAY 88

Do not run from your heavenly calling. When God gives you a task to complete, do not procrastinate in doing so. God will bless those that stay in alignment with their heavenly purpose in life.

- Jeremiah 17:13 King James Version (KJV)- 13 O Lord, the hope of Israel, all that forsake thee shall be ashamed, and they that depart from me shall be written in the earth, because they have forsaken the Lord...

Notes:

_____

_____

_____

_____

_____

_____

_____

_____

_____

_____

DAY 89

Have you ever asked God why me? Your negative experiences in life can help others. You never know what a person may be going through. Helping them to overcome their obstacles through your joyous persona and giving them advice on relevant previous experiences is well needed and worth it. Your gracious presence has the potential to brighten up the lives of others.

- Psalm 92:4-5 King James Version (KJV)- 4 For thou, Lord, hast made me glad through thy work: I will triumph in the works of thy hands. 5 O Lord, how great are thy works! and thy thoughts are very deep.

Notes:

_____

_____

_____

_____

_____

_____

_____

_____

_____

DAY 90

Investing a portion of your finances into the works of God will open a pathway of many blessings for you. God honors many people, especially those that can give a tenth of their financial income. This sacrifice shows that you are a good servant over your finances and you really love God. Do not be afraid to invest in your religious faith.

- Matthew 6:21 King James Version (KJV)- 21 For where your treasure is, there will your heart be also.

Notes:

_____

_____

_____

_____

_____

_____

_____

_____

_____

_____

WORDS TO REMEMBER

Do you know why you were created? God created you for a reason. That reason is connected to the works that he has designed for you to fulfill. Finding your purpose in life is very significant. Many people go through an entire lifetime longing to identify what they have been created and called to be or accomplish. I pray that you find your purpose in life. When you are made aware of your definite purpose and you start living in that purpose, a sense of fulfillment will begin to overtake you.

The sky is the limit for you. Never give up on your dreams. No matter how many times you are knocked down, DON'T GIVE UP! You can handle and overcome anything you direct your focus to, with the help of the Lord. He will never put more on you, than you are able to bare. Don't be afraid to embark upon new opportunities that God placed on heart.

Don't compare yourself to other people. You are an amazingly beautiful and gifted individual. Recognize and tap into your inner gifts. Those gifts were given specifically to you. God loves you so much that he set aside the best he has for you. Walk in humility, confidence and love. Remember that you are a great and unique blessing.

AFFIRMATIONS

Speak these affirmations over your life:

- I love you Lord.
- I will try to live my life so that you are pleased with me.
- I am great in your eyesight.
- I have been created in uniqueness.
- I will be successful.
- I will accomplish my goals.
- I will remain humble no matter how blessed I am or will become.
- My finances are blessed.
- My health is renewed and restored.
- My faith is strong.
- I will strive to take care of myself sufficiently.
- I am the head and not the tail.
- I am above and never beneath.
- I am more than a conqueror.
- I will not be defeated in any situation.
- I will not lack any necessities that I need in life.
- I will love and treat others with respect and dignity.
- I will help others in need, if I am able to do so.

I challenge you to add more affirmations to this list. Speak these affirmations over your life daily. Your tongue is very powerful. The more you positively speak into your atmosphere and life, the more those things that you speak will come to past.

PROPHETIC WORD

Reading this entire book, has shown God that you want to live your life as he has acknowledged for you to live through the ten commandments. God wants to reward you for the discipline and dedication you have exemplified by reading his word. I speak into your atmosphere, that many blessings are about to overtake your life. You will never lack or experience poverty, another day in your life. Persecution will no longer be your portion. Depression, worry and suicide will not affect you. Your mind, heart, spirit and soul has been officially and permanently renewed. You will receive answers and clarity on different issues you have prayed about. Have faith that this word will manifest in your life. Believe that God will take care of every need that you have. Be patient and watch God conduct magnificent works on your behalf. I pray that your pieces are no longer broken. Every piece that is associated and connected to you personally, will be made whole right now! Says the spirit of the Lord.

ABOUT THE AUTHOR

Ashley Monique has experienced many things in life. Through the ups and downs of life, she manages to push forward. Ashley is an author, entrepreneur, motivational speaker, facilitator and mentor that dedicates her life to Christ and serving others in need. She is a change agent in the community and very passionate about promoting holistic growth. Ashley is a believer in Jesus Christ, where she consistently studies the word of God. Ashley is a practicing member of the Christianity faith and is very proud to call herself a "Saved Christian Believer." No matter what she has been through, her grind to progress in life continues.

Ashley believes that obtaining a quality education is important. Currently, she is obtaining a PhD in Human and Social Services from Walden University. Before starting her doctoral program, Ashley was afforded the opportunity to receive a scholarship to attend the University of Alabama for her graduate studies. She graduated with honors, receiving a Master's Degree in Social Work. Her Bachelor's Degree in Arts and Sciences was received from Alabama State University with a focus in Social Work, as well. While at Alabama State University completing her undergraduate studies, she had the honor of being voted a campus queen during her freshman and sophomore year. Ashley was blessed and gracious enough to earn the Who's Who Among Students in American Universities and Colleges Award. This award allowed her to be recognized nationally, among an elite group of students. Ashley received the Outstanding Academic Achievement Award in Social Work and several Dean's List Awards for being an exceptional student throughout her collegiate years. In addition, Ashley had the opportunity to become an active member of the most prestigious sorority, Delta Sigma Theta Sorority, Incorporated.

Throughout the years, Ashley significantly focuses on the motto, "Never settle for being mediocre, always strive for greatness." With this motto in mind, Ashley obtained certifications to make herself more marketable in the work field. Ashley obtained a certification as an Associate Prevention Specialist through the Alabama Alcohol and Drug Abuse Association. She has been certified as an Associate Prevention Specialist for 11 years.

In addition, Ashley is certified as a Mental Health First Aid Instructor through the National Council for Behavioral Health. As a Mental Health First Aid Instructor, she certifies training participants as Mental Health First Aiders, through the facilitation of an 8-hour course.

Ashley had the honor of starting a business, where she serves as the Founder and Chief Executive Officer of a nonprofit organization. C.H.A.N.G.E. (Connecting Hands by Accommodating Necessary Growth for Everyone) is an established 501(c)(3) nonprofit organization that is geared towards serving individuals in need through providing services. The mission of C.H.A.N.G.E. is to enhance services and community mobilization through providing needed education, resources and mentorship to promote holistic growth for underprivileged families. The organizational objectives focus on community mobilization, community-based education, resources and mentorship.

Ashley has a strong passion for mentoring youth. Currently, she serves on the Board of Directors for Young Men on a Mission, a 501(c)(3) established nonprofit organization. This nonprofit organization was orchestrated and founded by Nick Rankins. Ashley has assisted with mentoring youth for over 10 years. The goal of this organization is to teach leadership and development skills to male adolescents. Through working with this program, she has had opportunities to assist with fundraising projects, community service projects, tutorial opportunities, educational and cultural experiences and college enrollment. She takes great delight in being an influence in the lives of our future leaders. Ashley was named "Volunteer of the Year" for her dedication and persistent work as a mentor, to this organization.

CPSIA information can be obtained
at www.ICGtesting.com
Printed in the USA
BVHW071932040819
555064BV00001B/213/P

9 781973 668565

CONDITIONAL LEGISLATION AND SUBORDINATE LEGISLATION

VOLUME 1, ISSUE 4 OF BRILLOPEDIA

VIVEK MALHOTRA

Publication

This research paper is published in volume 1, issue 4 of Brillopedia

CHAPTER ONE

ABSTRACT

One of the advances in the domain of authoritative cycle made during these days is that separated from 'unadulterated' regulatory capacity, the chief performs administrative capacity too. Because of various reasons, there is fast development of regulatory enactment. As per the customary hypothesis, the capacity of the leader is to manage the law sanctioned by the law making body, and in the ideal State, the administrative force must be practiced only by the officials who are straightforwardly dependable to the electorate. However, in truth, aside from 'unadulterated' authoritative capacities, the chief performs numerous administrative and legal capacities moreover. It has, thusly, been appropriately said that the designated enactment is incalculable to such an extent that a rule book would not exclusively be inadequate yet deceptive except if it be perused alongside assigned enactment which intensifies and supplements the tradition that must be adhered to. It is hard to give any exact meaning of the articulation 'designated legislation. It is similarly hard to state with sureness the extent of such appointed enactment. As indicated by Salmond, enactment is either incomparable or subordinate. Though the previous continues from sovereign or preeminent force, the last stream from any position other than the sovereign force, and is, in this manner, subordinate for its reality and duration on unrival or incomparable authority. Delegated enactment consequently is an enactment made by a body or individual other than the Sovereign in Parliament by righteousness of forces presented by such sovereign under the resolution. A basic importance of the articulation 'assigned enactment' might be given as: 'When the capacity of enactment is depended to organs other than the assembly by the governing body itself, the enactment made by such organs is called appointed enactment.'[1] The most important case relating to process of conditional legislation is HAMDARD DAWA KHANA VS UOI."

[1] AIR 1960 SC 554.

CHAPTER TWO

INTRODUCTION

Many factors are responsible for the rapid growth of delegated legislation in every modern democratic State. The traditional theory of 'laissez faire' has been given up by every State and the old 'police State' has now become a 'welfare State.' Because of this radical change in the philosophy as to the role to be played by the State, its functions have increased. Consequently, delegated legislation has become essential and inevitable.

1. Pressure upon Parliamentary Time: As a result of the expanding horizons of State activity, the bulk of legislation is so great that it is not possible for the legislature to devote sufficient time to discuss all the matters in detail. Therefore, legislature formulates the general policy and empowers the executive to fill in the details by issuing necessary rules, regulations, bye-laws, etc. In the words of Sir CECIL CARR, delegated legislation is "a growing child called upon to relieve the parent of the strain of overwork and capable of attending to minor matters, while the parent manages the main business."

2. Technicality: Sometimes, the subject-matter on which legislation is required is so technical in nature that the legislator, being himself a common man, cannot be

expected to appreciate and legislate on the same, and the assistance of experts may be required. Members of Parliament may be the best politicians but they are not experts to deal with highly technical matters which are required to be handled by the experts. Here the legislative power may be conferred on expert to deal with the technical problems, e.g. gas, atomic -energy, drugs, electricity, etc."

3. Flexibility: At the time of passing any legislative enactment, it is impossible to foresee all the contingencies, and some provision is required to be made for these unforeseen situations demanding exigent action. A legislative amendment is a slow and cumbersome process, but by the device

of delegated legislation, the executive can meet the situation expeditiously, e.g. bank-rate, police regulation export and import, foreign exchange, etc. For that purpose, in many statutes, a 'removal of difficulty' clause is found empowering the administration overcome difficulties by exercising delegated power."

4. Experiment: The practice of delegated legislation enables the executive to experiment. This method permits rapid utilization of experience and implementation of necessary changes in application of the provisions in the light of such experience, e.g. in road traffic matters, an experiment may be conducted and in the light of its application necessary changes could be made. Delegated legislation thus allows employment and application of past experience."

5. Emergency: In times of emergency, quick action is required to be taken. The legislative process is note quipped to provide for urgent solution to meet the situation. Delegated legislation is the only convenient remedy. Therefore, in times of war and other national emergencies, such as aggression, break -down of law and order, strike, 'bandh', etc. the executive is vested with special and extremely wide powers to deal with the situation. There was substantial growth of delegated legislation during the two World Wars. Similarly, in situation of epidemics, floods, inflation, economic depression, etc. immediate remedial actions are necessary which may not be possible by lengthy legislative process and delegated legislation is the only convenient remedy."

6. Complexity of Modern Administration: The complexity of modem administration and the expansion of the functions of the State to the economic and social sphere have rendered it necessary to resort to new forms of legislation and to give wide powers to various authorities on suitable occasions. By resorting to traditional legislative process, the entire object may be frustrated by vested interests and the goal of control and regulation over private trade and business may not be achieved at all. The practice of empowering the executive to make subordinate legislation within the prescribed sphere has evolved out of practical necessity and pragmatic needs of the modem welfare State.[1]"

[1]https://thefactfactor.com/facts/law/civil_law/administrative-law/ growth-of-delegated-legislation/4262/

CHAPTER THREE

CLASSIFICATION OF ADMINISTRATIVE RULE-MAKING POWER OR DELEGATED LEGISLATION

Administrative rule-making or delegated legislation in India is commonly expressed by the term "statutory rules and orders". However, this classification is not exhaustive as it appears in other forms also, i.e. regulation, notification, bye-law, scheme and direction. These terminologies are confusing because different words are used for the same thing and same words are used for different things."

Title- Based Classification:

1. RULE: The term "rule" is defined in the General Clauses Act, 1897 as a rule made in exercise of power conferred by any enactment and shall include a regulation made as a "rule" under any enactment. These rules may be made applicable to a particular individual or to a general public. It may include rules of procedures as under the Atomic Energy Act, 1948, and also the rules of substantive law."

2. REGULATIONS: This term is not confined to delegated legislation. It means an instrument by which decisions, orders and acts of the government are made known to public. But in the sphere of administrative rule making, the term relates to a situation where power is given to fix the date for the enforcement of an Act, or to grant exemptions from the Act or to fix prices, etc."

3. ORDER: This term is used to cover various forms of legislative and quasi-judicial decisions. Orders may be specific or general. The former

Thus, when the delegate is given the power of making rules and regulations in order to fill in the details to carry out and sub serve the purposes of the legislation, the manner in which the requirements of the statute are to be met and the rights created therein to be enjoyed, ids an exercise of delegated legislation.[3]"

But when the legislation is complete in itself and the legislature has itself made the law and the only function left to the delegate is to apply the law to an area or to determine the time and manner of carrying it into effect it is conditional legislation."

Hamdard Dawakhana V. Union of India. To put in the language of American case Field and Co. v. Clark.[4]

To assert that a law is less than a law because it is made to depend upon a future event or act to rob the legislature of the power to act wisely for the public welfare whenever a law is passed relating to a state of affairs not yet developed or the things future and impossible to fully know."

The proper distinction was pointed out in this case thus: "The legislature cannot delegate its power to make a law, but it can make to a law delegate a power to determine some fact or state of things upon which the law makes or intends to make its own action depend."There are many things upon which wise and useful legislation must depend which cannot be known to the law making power and must, therefore, be subject of enquiry and determination outside the hall of legislature."

[1] 3 App CAS 889, (1877-78) LR 3 App CAS 889, [1878] UKPC 1, [1873] 3 AC 889, [1878] UKPC 26

[2] AIR 1943 Cal 285

[3] 1998 232 ITR 908 Patna

[4]1960 AIR 554, 1960 SCR (2) 671

CHAPTER FIVE

CONSTITUIONALITY OF DELEGATED LEGILATION

The question generally arises whether any limitations or checks have - been laid down under the Indian Constitution against the delegation of powers by the legislature to an outside authority. As a matter of fact, in a state having a written constitution which forms the fundamental and paramount law of the nation, the legislature must act within the ambit of the powers defined by the constitution and subject to the limitations prescribed thereby. Every Parliamentary Actor the legislation which is against or contrary to the provisions of the Constitution is null and void, and the duty of keeping the legislature within its bounds, in system incorporating the doctrine of judicial review, devolves upon the courts. Our Indian Constitution incorporate the doctrine of judicial review of legislation as to its conformity with the constitution. On the other -hand, there is no written constitution in England which circumscribes the powers of Parliament which is sovereign in the eyes of law. There does not exist in any part of the British Empire any person or body of persons, executive, legislative or judicial, which can pronounce void any enactment passed by the British Parliament on the ground of such enactment being opposed to the Constitution, or on any ground whatever, except, of course it is being repealed by Parliament. The British Constitution has entrusted to the two Houses of Parliament, subject to the assent of the King, on absolute power untrammelled by any written instrument obedience to which may be compelled by some judicial body. Parliament may accordingly delegate to any extent its powers of law-making to an outside authority. As a matter of law, Parliament may surrender all its power in favour of another body as it actually did in 1807, when the English and Scottish Parliament passed Acts of Union providing for the coming into existence of a new body, Parliament of Great Britain. The limits of delegate legislation in the English Constitution, if there are to be any, must, therefore, remain a question of policy and not a justiciable issue for the courts.[1]"

[1]   https://researchers.mq.edu.au/en/publications/rethinking-the-constitutionality-of-delegated-legislation

CHAPTER SIX

OCCURENCES OF CONDITIONAL LEGISLATION

1. The assembly engages the chief to extend the movement of a current law to a particular zone or district."
2. To decide and choose the hour of use of an Act to a given zone."
3. To widen the range of a Temporary Act, subject to most extreme period fixed by the authoritative gathering.
4. To decide and choose the degree and cut off points inside which the rule or Act should be employable and usable."
5. Finally, to present an extraordinary law if the considered circumstance has emerged in the assessment of the administration."

Conditional Legislation permits better usage and better reach of laws as it gives them plentiful prudence to work and to settle on choices with respect to execution in the most ideal way. Along these lines, all the cutting edge financial government assistance plans are an arrangement of the law making body, however they have gotten effective in the nation on account of their usage. All the "when, where and how" parts of execution have been ticked liberally by the administration as a result of the watchfulness that they have been given by the assembly for the usage of the Acts surrounded by the legislators. However, this attentiveness can't be practiced past the force that has been designated. Whenever surpassed, at that point that activity is invalid and void.[1]"

[1]DR N. V. PARANJAPE Studies in Jurisprudence and Legal Theory, 8th Edition, Central Law Agency

CHAPTER SEVEN

CATEGORIES OF CONDITIONAL LEGISLATION"

1. In the main class, when the Legislature has finished the assignment of ordering a Statute, the whole structure of the enactment is prepared however its future propriety to a given district is left to the emotional fulfilment of the agent who being satisfied and fulfilled about the conditions demonstrating the right an ideal opportunity for applying the arrangements of the said Act to a given area practices that power as a representative of the parent authoritative body. Right when the Act itself is done and is endorsed to be reliably applied in future to every single one of the people who are to be made sure about by the extent of the Act, the Legislature can be said to have finished its assignment. This would be a demonstration of straightforward as can be restrictive enactment relying on the abstract fulfilment of the representative concerning when the said Act authorized and finished by the parent Legislature is to be made successful."

2. The second classification of restrictive enactments wherein the representative needs to choose whether and under what conditions a finished Act of the parent enactment which has just come into power is to be halfway pulled back from activity in a given territory or in given cases so as not to be material to a given class of people who are generally in fact administered by the Act. In such sort of cases, the representative needs to act adversely by pulling back the working demonstration, completely or somewhat because of any reasons for activity of administration."

3. The third classification of cases wherein the activity of contingent enactment would rely on fulfilment of the agent in target realities set by one class of people looking for advantage of such an activity so as to deny the

adversary class of people who in any case may have just got legal advantages under the Act and who are probably going to lose the current advantage on account of activity of such a force by the representative. In such kind of cases the fulfilment of the representative has essentially to be founded on target thought of the pertinent information for and against the activity of such force."

The milestone case for designation of enactment is the Re : Delhi Laws Act Case [4], which spun around the topic of in the case of giving the Lt. Lead representative the ability to broaden the use of law is designation of intensity? Privy committee saw that Indian assembly isn't a specialist or representative however was expected to have whole powers of enactment and of a similar sort of the parliament itself. It was seen that Indian council had practiced its judgment regarding the spot, individual, law, powers and what the lead representative was needed to do was to make it endless supply of specific conditions. This is called restrictive enactment which was maintained by the court. In JATINDRA NATH v. Territory of BIHAR, it was held that there could be no designated enactment in India past contingent enactment.[1]"

[1]https://www.lawyersclubindia.com/articles/Conditional-legislation-and-delegated-legislation-1126.asp

AIR 1951 SC 347.

http://www.manupatra.com/roundup/333/Articles/In%20re%20Delhi%20Laws%20Act%20Case.pdf

Lightning Source UK Ltd.
Milton Keynes UK
UKHW020647280122
397869UK00009B/518